The Profit Recipe

THE PROFIT RECIPE

TOP RESTAURANT TRENDS AND HOW TO USE THEM TO BOOST YOUR MARGINS

by

CESAR QUINTERO

FOODPRENEUR / COACH / SPEAKER

MENU

Message from My Soap Box 7

Chapter 1: "The Big 5" 11
5 Biggest Mistakes I Made When I Started
Summary
Bonus Action Items
- ❖ Tips for Growing Revenues With Minimum Investment
- ❖ Hiring for Now and Later: Employee Retention

Reflection

Chapter 2: Really??? 41
The Realities of Running a Food Business in the 21st Century
Summary
Bonus Action Items
- ❖ 4 Ways To Maximize Your Margins Now
- ❖ Are You and Your Employees On Top of Your KPIs?

Reflection

Chapter 3: Call a Psychic 67
Where Is the Food Industry Headed?
Summary
Bonus Action Items
- ❖ How Generation Y and Z Are Shifting the Industry

Reflection

Chapter 4: The Profit Recipe **89**
   How to Boost Your Margins Using the Food Industry's Top Trends
   Summary
   Bonus Action Items
   - *How You Can Turn Problems Into Profits*
   - *How To Negotiate With Food Vendors*
   - *Keep Your Menu Fresh by Staying Ahead of Trends*
   - *5 Reasons to Add a Delivery Component Business*
   - *7 Questions Before Implementing a Delivery Service*
   - *4 Advantages of an Online Ordering System*
   - *Rev Up Sales With a User-Friendly Online Ordering*
   - *4 Things Food Trucks Can Teach Us About Innovation*
   - *5 Tips for Building Your Restaurant's Marketing Plan*
   - *10 Social Media Strategies to Market Your Restaurant*
   - *Use Content Marketing to Cultivate Relationships*
   Reflection

Chapter 5: The Time Is Now! **149**
   2020 Is Closer Than It Seems

Chapter 6: The Profit Recipe Action Items! **153**
   Ingredients for Success

Acknowledgements **155**

Message From My Soap Box

The food industry sucks: it sucks money, energy and time, leaving owners with very little rewards in return.

Why is it that the first thing that comes to most people's mind when starting a business is to open a restaurant or enter the food industry? I serve as the perfect example: Having graduated as a production engineer and worked in marketing for a Fortune 100 consumer products company, one day I decided to quit my job and start my own business—a food business.

Maybe it's because we eat three or more times a day that makes us experts in the field, or a perceived notion that restaurants always make money, because, hey... we all have to eat, right? Has anyone truly correlated the poor statistics for startups with the fact that food businesses represent a large portion of these new businesses?

Having owned and managed a successful food business for almost a decade now, I can provide some insight and experiences that unfortunately took too long to realize. I'm sad to admit that we're no longer in the golden age of restaurants. It has become a "penny pinching" business. According to the National Restaurant Association and Deloitte & Touche LLP, the average net profit before taxes for restaurants currently varies between 2 and 6 percent depending on the type. Even in the proven franchise world, the average food franchisee earns less than 5% net profit before taxes, according to a study from Franchise Business Review. That's less than $50,000 on a $1,000,000 operation!

I am aware that I may sound like a negative Nancy, but I would have loved for someone to tell me these things before I invested my life's savings and time in the business. And that's why I decided to write this book.

I'm glad to report that not only did my business survive the past decade, it thrived in the economic downturn by focusing on creating a niche market based on trends to grow sales and controlling the back end with systems and processes that helped me DOUBLE the industry standard net profit. In contrast, my competitors were focused on pure growth instead of profitability. They were spending money like crazy. Eventually, most had to sell or close due to cash flow and debt issues.

My business, Fit2Go, is one of the leading healthy meal delivery services in South Florida, with over 25,000 registered customers, delivering over 1,000 meals daily. At the same time, I also developed our own proprietary food delivery software, Fit2Go Delivery System (Fit2Go DS), a platform used by other food businesses to increase profitability. It is my life's work and my contribution to others in the food industry to help them achieve the freedom and results they want in their marketplace.

The purpose of this book is to reach all restaurateurs, food establishment operators or anyone who is thinking of starting a food business. I want to share with you my experiences in the hopes that I can save you from making the same mistakes I did. I also want to share how I took advantage of the current food trends and where I see the market headed, so you can make your restaurant more profitable and stand out against your competitors.

You'll learn how the food industry can be one of the most rewarding, fun, and challenging businesses to be in for those of us willing to work hard, but most importantly, work smart.

So let's get started with The Profit Recipe!

CHAPTER 1: THE BIG 5

The 5 Biggest Mistakes I Made When I Started

When I started Fit2Go in 2004, I didn't have any experience running a restaurant, and I'm not sure why I thought I was prepared for it either. Without realizing it, I had to quickly become a jack of all trades: a part-time sales person, customer service representative, delivery guy, and dessert maker... It was just me and the chef. Fast forward to 2015 and Fit2Go is one of the leading healthy meal delivery services in South Florida.

However, it didn't come easily and I have had more than my fair share of big mistakes and sleepless nights. This chapter focuses on the Top 5 mistakes I made when starting my business. For those of you contemplating starting your new food business, this chapter will suggest key strategic points to help you jumpstart into profitability. If you already own and operate a food business, you will surely relate to my stories, but pay close attention just in case you are still stuck on one of them. If you have others to add to the list, use #TheProfitRecipe and join our community so we all share our experiences!

Mistake #1: Building out my brand new kitchen

This was a costly mistake. When I look back at it now, I'm surprised that I was able to survive it, but I guess that's where being a passionate and naive entrepreneur can be an asset. If you're like most 1st time restaurateurs, there is a strong tendency to want to have everything "shiny and new" versus using what's already available. In this case, I wanted to build my own kitchen so I could design it the way I wanted. I thought it would be cheaper and help me control the quality.

Big mistake. I didn't understand how long the permitting process would take. I had estimated it at 6 months, as most consultants said. In reality, it took 18 months. That was 18 months paying rent, AND I wasn't able to sell one single meal. Ouch. During that time, instead of growing my business and making money, I spent my days learning about contracting and permitting while dealing with what I like to call the "7 Departments from Hell": Electrical, Plumbing, Building, Mechanical, Sewer, Zoning and Fire. I spent my days waiting on inspectors and filling out paperwork. Every inspector had his own interpretation of the code and the specifications of one department didn't match with others.

The other item I became very familiar with during this process was the grease trap, which is required for every kitchen. A grease trap is a receptacle that filters out all the grease from your restaurant before it flows into the city sewer system. This cost me $30,000 alone. Talk to any restaurateur and mention that you had to install a new grease trap and you will surely get some sympathy, and perhaps a free drink or two out of it. Are you starting to get the picture? Bottom line is that had I known these things beforehand, I would have found a faster or cheaper alternative so I could have spent those first 18 months selling rather than being a contractor.

Take away

Find an existing kitchen. It can be a restaurant that has gone out of business or a kitchen you can lease. You can even sublease from an operating facility. Make sure that whichever option you choose already has all of the proper permits. Don't forget to ask about the condition of the grease trap. You may spend more than you want initially to get a space that already has everything done for you and it may not be exactly as you want, but it will save you time, money, and heartache in the long run.

If you have your heart set on building your own kitchen, do it once you've got your business up, running and making money so you aren't trying to do everything at once. Also make sure you have enough cash flow to hire a contractor to manage your build out so you can focus on running your business versus learning about the permitting process.

Mistake #2: Thinking that once I launched, the sales would start rolling in.

I had a background in consumer products and brand marketing in a big corporate environment where we had huge budgets for mass marketing. When I started Fit2Go, I used some of those same strategies and spent a lot of money buying mass media packages in TV and radio. Once I finally got all my permits and was ready to start selling, I thought that people would easily be able to find me and that the orders would just start rolling in. I believed that because I had this website which could take orders, I would immediately start generating revenue to help me recoup my investment thus far and start paying for all my expenses. WRONG!

Launching a business and making money from your business are two very different things. While I had great branding and beautiful, professional materials, I didn't have a plan in place to identify what our target audiences wanted and how we were going to reach them. I learned that in order to sell my product, people needed to try it or get a recommendation in order to convert.

But social media had not yet picked up when I started my business. Some of you may remember that marketing through word of mouth effectively and measurably was more difficult back then. So I shifted my strategy and started hustling and giving free samples out, knocking on doors, leaving flyers everywhere and promoting my website. A tipping point that really helped me was my partnership with Groupon, which was just getting started. I had read about them in Inc. Magazine and contacted them because I saw the potential of word of mouth and sampling at a higher level. Fit2Go became the second Groupon deal in Miami.

All of this helped us kick-start our sales effort. Mind you, I said sales—not profits. We'll talk about this more in mistake #3. Bottom line is that just because you build it, doesn't mean they will come. You need to have a detailed plan on how to reach your target audience, convert them, and keep them coming back.

Take away

You have to have a marketing and sales plan in place from the start, and you must factor in the time it's going to take to build awareness for your business and to generate orders. I also do not believe mass media is useful for small businesses. We need to generate sales, not branding. Track and measure all your campaigns and find at least 5 different ways to reach your target market. Only by tracking can you validate whether a campaign was a good return on investment or not. While branding is important, generating sales in a profitable manner is key. A successful marketing campaign has to pay for its cost after taking into account the cost of goods sold. Make sure you allocate appropriate resources to this endeavor and cut marketing spend on campaigns that don't return more than you put in.

- ❖ *For more helpful hints on growing revenues with minimal investment, check out the bonus action items (<u>on page #25</u>)*
  (at the end of this chapter)!

Mistake #3: Not understanding discounts and how long it takes to make money

As I mentioned in Mistake #2, once I had a sales plan and started hustling, I was able to generate sales and start to build a customer database, but I was doing it at a loss by giving away FREE samples and offering steep discounts. While this worked from a sales perspective, those dollars were hitting neither my bottom line nor my pocket. Those sales did help get the word out which led to more sales, but it took a while for me to start making a profit and I had not really considered this when I started the business.

I focused on volume until I got to a point where I could really look at costs and start to focus on profitability. Over time, I was able to raise prices while maintaining a big portion of those customers so I became profitable. But if I had not been capitalized properly, I wouldn't have been able to stay in business. I was also learning along the way what pricing strategy made sense for my business, which was still a new, disruptive model at the time.

I learned that price should be dictated by the market and not by my costs. I was underselling my product to gain volume, but I later realized that even when I raised my prices 30%, most of my clients stayed. To date, our rates are above those of my direct competitors, yet our target market perceives value from our service. Find your niche market and give them what they ask for and they will pay for it. More on this in Chapter #4.

Actually, even if you feel that you will lose customers by raising your price, consider the following study from ActionCOACH®: If you have a gross margin of 25% (as most restaurants do), when you raise prices 10%, you can lose up to 33% of your customers and you will still be making the same profit! Isn't that insane? It seems counterintuitive yet it's true, do the math! Do you think a third of your customers would leave if you charge them $11 instead of $10 for a product that fits their needs? The rest would just go straight to your bottom line!

Take away

Make sure you are properly capitalized while you build the business. I needed 24 months of working capital before I hit the breakeven point in cash flow. Everyone thinks that they will be different and they will start making money sooner, but that's why we see so many restaurants go out of business in the first year. Even the places that have great food, great service, and a great location, right? If you don't have working capital while you are building up the volume, you will be hard pressed to stay in business.

Have the right pricing strategy dictated by the market and your target customer. Don't be afraid to raise prices if you're under market. Never discount! Always try to give something on top that is of value to your target customer and of low cost to you. For example, offer a complimentary glass of wine to anyone who orders a special in your menu. It's a high perceived value to them at a low cost to you.

Mistake #4: Working with only one vendor

I had no food business experience when I started, so I asked a friend in the restaurant business who I should use for my food supplier and they suggested Sysco. I called Sysco and they helped us plan the menu and determine the different ingredients we needed. Voila! I had a food vendor that I came to rely on heavily and they were, still are by the way, great. But once I started looking at profitability, I realized that there was a huge opportunity there.

For one, I wasn't even comparing our pricing to other vendors. I just compared it to retail, which made the pricing I was getting look pretty good. I was just automatically purchasing our ingredients on a weekly basis without questioning the costs. Big mistake. My food cost was close to 40% when it should have been between 28–32%. This was my biggest expense, yet it was at the bottom of the list of what I was focused on. I was busy with sales, food delivery, customer service, employees—all important things—but at the expense of my biggest cost.

Once I realized this, my engineering background kicked in, and I added a food cost analysis for each meal and portion to Fit2Go DS so I knew exactly how much everything cost. I also built a bidding system for all our ingredients to use with vendors so I could create a competitive environment that benefited the business. Food costs can change dramatically from week to week, so this process helped us get the best price each week. The result was a decrease of $150k in the first year and a food cost margin of 30% of sales (right on target!)

Take away

Use at least 2 or 3 different vendors. For negotiation purposes, you can allow a vendor to have 70%+ of your purchase if they agree to a fixed cost-plus model and check them versus your other vendors on a weekly basis. Know what your margins are. Create a system to look at all your costs on a periodic basis (remember all produce and protein prices change weekly!) and make sure you are always comparing prices to other vendors.

Mistake #5: Hiring friends and family

This was probably the toughest mistake I learned as a business owner. When I started my company, I had lots of friends and family working with me. Not only that, but every time we would hire, it would be a friend or family member of an employee. We even got to the point where we had an employee's husband, mother and brother in-law working together! I didn't realize how important it was to have people on my team that had restaurant and food experience. I figured since I didn't have any restaurant experience, no one else needed to either. It was great until it wasn't.

In the beginning, I had the same mentality as an employee. Like the rest of the team, I was thinking I should be earning more, wondering why I was working so hard, and asking myself why I was frustrated with my boss, which was ME! I didn't view myself as the leader that I needed to be. Big mistake. Everyone started having their own vision of what my company needed to be and how it should grow versus me creating and sharing my vision and then making sure everyone on the team embraced it.

Luckily, I became involved with the Entrepreneur Organization (EO) Accelerator program, and I had an AHA moment: I needed to focus ON the business and not get consumed with day-to-day operations. I needed to create processes and systems for others to do the work so I could focus on the strategic growth of the company.

I created our mission, vision and values for my company and realized I had some people on our team that didn't fit that culture and thus I was going to have to let them go. One of those people was my best friend. Believe me that those relationships are really tested when you realize that they are not the right fit for the business, culture, or position they hold. It was not fair to my company or to them to keep them around. A "C" player in your company may be an "A" player in another company. It's all about culture and fit. It benefits no one to keep an employee on when they aren't the right person for the company. I had to step up and be the leader, which I did. I'm thankful for everyone who pitched in during those early days, but I did them all a disservice by not setting them up for success and making sure they were the right fit for the company.

Take away

Create your mission, vision and values early and make sure the people you hire have those values. If they don't, don't hire them no matter how much experience they have or how they are related to you. Remember, you are the leader, so act like one. If your culture isn't working, look no further than yourself and change it. If you end up hiring friends or family, make sure they understand your vision and culture. Set ground rules and clear boundaries to avoid any misunderstandings along the way. Get yourself in a group with other like-minded entrepreneurs who can help you see things you can't because you are too busy working IN your business rather than ON it.

- ❖ *For more helpful hints on hiring and retaining employees, check out the bonus action items (on page #30) (at the end of this chapter)!*

Chapter 1 Summary

Mistake #1: Building out my kitchen versus leasing space

Key Learning: Find an existing kitchen that already has permits you need. Rent, sub-lease or share the space until your volume permits.

Mistake #2: Thinking once I launched, the sales would start rolling in

Key Learning: Have a plan in place to reach your target audiences. Measure all campaigns and only use the ones that have ROI.

Mistake #3: Not realizing how long it would take to make money

Key Learning: Use market price. Don't discount! Always add value through low cost add-ons. Have at least 18 months of working capital to support your growth.

Mistake #4: Working with only one vendor

Key Learning: Know your food costs and get quotes from multiple vendors on a frequent basis.

Mistake #5: Hiring friends and family

Key Learning: Develop your mission, vision and values and hire your team based on that. If they don't have your values or embrace your mission and vision, they shouldn't be on your team.

Chapter 1 Bonus Action Items

This material expands on the ideas discussed in:

- ❖ Mistake #2: Thinking that once I launched, the sales would start rolling in
- ❖ Mistake #5: Hiring family and friends

Helpful Tips for Growing Revenues With Little Investment

1. Rely on word of mouth

We all know there is no better recommendation than a personal referral. To drive customers into your location, you need to get people talking. How? By treating them well. Good customer service goes a long way in promoting word of mouth—and good customer service can set you apart from the competition.

When someone dines at your restaurant and has a positive experience, he or she will more than likely mention it at the office. A coworker then emails four of her girlfriends and they all have lunch with you. Then, two of the girlfriends talk about it at a party. Those party goers decide to take their spouse or family out for a night on the town…you see where this is going, don't you?

A simple referral or loyalty program can help motivate your loyal customers to recommend you to others.

2. Take advantage of free tools like social media

This might seem simple, and you probably already have a social media site or two set up for your restaurant (Facebook, LinkedIn, Twitter, etc.), but the key to success with this strategy is keeping the content fresh—just like your ingredients!

This is FREE advertising, so use it to its fullest potential! Share pictures of your best dishes. Encourage patrons to check in while dining—offer incentives for them to do so. Ask yourself if you're making it interesting to your followers. Are you enticing them to keep returning to see what's new?

While the cost is free, social media is still an investment. It will require someone's time—either yours or a staff member's—but it will pay back in profit ten-fold if you're able to capture and keep people's attention. Make a scheduled commitment to providing updates on a consistent basis. Keep it fresh and your following will devour it.

3. Get involved

Your restaurant is a local establishment. You are part of a local community. So get involved in the community and inspire people to patronize your restaurant. This means participating in events such as festivals, food tastings, non-profit fundraisers and the like. All of these scenarios make it possible for future loyal customers to taste a sampling of your food, or experience a positive interaction with your staff or representatives, and become inspired to grace your booths. This will also get them talking (word of mouth, remember?). It will help fill your seats and grow your food profits.

4. Learn who the food critics are, where they are and how to talk to them to get an A+ review

What is it that makes the world go round? Is it love? Is it music? No, it's not even food. It is connections. In this business, and most other businesses for that matter, it's all about who you know. Years ago, restaurant reviewers in the newspaper were the go-to source for learning about new restaurants. However, they only reviewed certain restaurants, and they would typically review them only one time. This meant that many eateries out there simply didn't get the recognition they deserved. They survived on word of mouth alone.

Today, there is a hybrid of the old school newspaper restaurant reviewer and word of mouth. They are known as food bloggers, and they have the potential to be some of your best friends. You should certainly factor them into your marketing strategy. The internet is full of countless food blogs, and you can be sure that even a small city probably has quite a few of them. How do you get to know them though? It is actually quite simple.

a. *Identifying local bloggers*

First, start looking up food bloggers in your area and make a list of them. When you are making your list, include all of the food bloggers around, including those that may specialize in blogs about wine, beer, spirits or even desserts. You may also be able to entice them if you have the food and drink they enjoy. Make sure they have people commenting, liking or sharing their posts. You want to choose influencers that have a following, even if it's a little small.

When you are learning about the bloggers, you need to do more than just make a list of people to contact. Actually take the time to read the blog and understand what they do. If you have an Italian restaurant, you probably do not want to reach out to a food blogger who specializes only in Asian cuisine. You also do not want to connect with a blogger who only trashes the restaurants and eateries he or she reviews.

    b. *Building meaningful relationships with food bloggers*

Read the blog to make sure you'd be a good fit for one another before you try connect with them through their comments or contact info. If you decide they're a good fit, send them a polite email and mention their name as well as their blog. This shows that you actually paid attention and did your homework. Let them know why you reached out to them in particular and why you would like to work with them. They are looking for content, and you are looking for exposure.

Invite him or her to dine at your restaurant, just as newspaper reviewers would have done. You might want to invite them to dinner, to a special event or give them a pass to come into the restaurant at a time of their choosing.

It is important that you stress the fact that even though they may be eating free at your restaurant, there are no strings attached. They do not have to provide you with a glowing review just because you provided them with a meal. You are looking for honesty. This helps them retain their integrity and the trust of their audience. When you wow them with a great meal and great service, chances are good that they will write a positive review anyway.

Once you have a few popular bloggers who are eating at your restaurant and writing about it, you might just start to see your clientele start to rise. They can get the word out about your eatery, and the more that's written about your restaurant the higher it can rank in the search engines. It's a win-win for everyone!

Hiring for Now and Later: A Look at Restaurant Employee Retention

Working in an industry famous for its turnover rate—recent stats place it at higher than 90 percent, which is one of the worst in any industry—makes employee retention an important concern. We already know that hiring our friends and family can be a costly mistake because we read Mistake #5 earlier in this chapter, but they're not the only people you may have to part ways with. Every dollar we put into finding, hiring, training and paying new hires can seem like a waste once they're gone, so what can we reduce employee turnover and the associated costs?

1. Support employees who are struggling

The service industry can be harsh. Everyone from you on down to your lowest-level staffers are at the mercy of your customers. How well someone's night goes may very well hinge on the internal temperature of a steak. The truth is that employees are often working in high-stress situations, so take the time to show your staff you support and appreciate them—even when things go wrong. Sometimes a few well-chosen, well-timed and sincere words of praise or your willingness to help get food out when a line gets too long can prevent a fed-up employee from calling it quits.

2. Involve your employees in staffing decisions

What kind of help do you need right now? What is missing? Once you have the answers, sit with your most seasoned employees and create a system of processes, a hierarchy of leadership and a strategy for mentorship for any new employees you hire. They know exactly what's going on, what shifts could use less hands and which can use more. They'll help you make sure you always have the help you need without overstaffing.

3. Establish a training period and develop a detailed training manual for all new hires

Retention is cheaper than recruiting, so train all new hires in all of the basic positions when they begin, no matter what role they will fill. Not only will they feel like there's room for advancement, they'll also be able to pitch in when one of your teams needs help because they already know what to do.

4. Provide growth opportunities

The food and beverage industry has been suffering from a shortage of meaningful, long-term career paths for some time now. Don't make the mistake of assuming that your new employee is just there for the summer. Always communicate opportunities for advancement to every member of your staff. You may be surprised who steps up to the plate. Build milestones into each employee's plan for growth and find ways to incentivize them. Sit down periodically—even once or twice a year—and review their progress to keep their momentum and motivation going strong.

5. Identify critical job stressors

What causes stress among your staff? Once you're able to identify them, you'll be able to develop plans for how to handle each stressor and reduce team anxiety. Have veteran staff members conduct a professional development activity where they model how to handle a variety of common issues. Not only will this prepare everyone to deal with them in real life, it will build camaraderie and a support network between members of your staff.

6. Improve in-house communication

Make sure your managers are effective communicators. If not, find ways to help them develop their skills. A person can't be an effective manager and motivator if he or she is unable to communicate.

Take Away

The reality is that your employees are less likely to jump ship if they feel respected, appreciated and productive. Employee retention is an ongoing process that needs to become an ingrained part of your business. You should get so used to praising employees who deserve it when they deserve it that you no longer look at it as employee retention—it's just what you do.

Chapter 1 Reflection

WHAT WILL YOU TAKE FROM THIS CHAPTER TO ADAPT TO YOUR PROFIT RECIPE?

_____

_____

_____

WHAT ARE THE TOP 3 ACTIONS YOU ARE GOING TO TAKE AS A RESULT OF THIS CHAPTER?

1. _____

   _____

2. _____

   _____

3. _____

   _____

CHAPTER 2: REALLY???

The Realities of Running a Food Business in the 21st Century

There may have been a time when it was easy to make money in the restaurant business. In fact, I've heard that during the '70s, '80s and '90s, restaurants were a high-margin business. If you had a restaurant, you really didn't have to worry about portion sizes, food control and labor costs because margins were plentiful. Unfortunately, this is no longer the reality, but rather the exception. Really, you might ask? Consider that food costs are up

105% in the last decade. Labor costs continue to rise with no end in sight. Add regulations, inflation, taxes, fuel costs, competition, etc., etc. You get the picture.

In this chapter, I will share some of the cold hard facts about the food industry today, and how I applied my profit recipe to help you deal with them. If you are already running a restaurant and have been feeling pinched for a while, this chapter will give you some comfort knowing you are not alone and it will provide some avenues to improve your profitability.

Reality #1: Margins are extremely tight

Food costs, labor costs, and energy costs have all increased dramatically over the last 10 years, and customers want to pay less and less for their food.

Food costs alone have gone up 105% in the last 10 years, and are expected to double within the next 5! As an example, according to the USDA, fresh vegetable prices jumped 5% in 2013 alone, and are forecasted to rise ~3% in 2014. That's 8.2% compounded in just 2 years!

The other key reality is that food today is a global business. The majority of shrimp comes from India, fish comes from China and limes from Mexico. So if there is a weather catastrophe, like a tsunami in India, it has an impact on food prices in United States, even at the local sourcing level. Recently there was a lime shortage in Mexico and the price of limes everywhere skyrocketed for about 6 weeks from $15/case to $110+/case! We were able to substitute lemons for limes for a while but we weren't the only ones, so then lemon prices went through the roof because of demand. It's a crazy commodities business. If you don't have a plan in place that gives you flexibility or if your menu can't sustain those changes, you're going to be severely challenged.

The same can be said about energy prices and labor costs. We've all heard about Seattle passing legislation that will gradually raise the city's minimum wage to $15 per hour and tie it to inflation. With labor costs accounting for between 25 to 35 percent of a restaurant's total sales, any increase in wages will have a big impact on profitability. Given that the last minimum wage increase was in July 2009, we can safely assume there will be an increase soon.

The U.S. Energy Information Administration (EIA) expects the U.S. annual average electricity price to increase 3.1% in 2014, which would be the highest growth rate since 2008, primarily in response to higher fuel costs for power generation. The largest price increases generally occur in the Northeast region, where it is projected that prices will increase by an additional 2.4% during 2015. That's 5%+ in 1 year!

Margins are tight in the restaurant industry and I don't see any reprieve any time soon. It's a reality that truly "bites" into your profits and you need to be conscious so you can plan accordingly.

Take away

Focus on growing your volume. You need to have volume first in order to sustain your business. But then,

MUST DO!!

very quickly be sure you've got the processes and systems on the back end to control costs. Otherwise you're just growing at a loss and spinning your wheels. Remember in Chapter 1 we discussed this?

Create good systems and processes. Automate as many of your processes as you can so you can do more with less. Create a repeatable system for everything so you don't need a highly-educated, high-priced employee to do it. This is where my engineering background really helped: I created a software platform, Fit2Go DS, to manage all aspects of my business so I didn't need as many employees. Fit2Go DS also helped me track and measure data in order to make better management decisions. Remember in Chapter 1 how I was able to save 150k in food costs by pricing every recipe and implementing a weekly bidding process with my vendors? That was because the platform helped me accomplish this with almost no labor on a weekly basis.

Find and join a restaurant buying group. A buying group is an entity that is created to leverage the purchasing power of several restaurants to obtain discounts from vendors based on the collective buying power of the members. Food suppliers feed off independently owned restaurants that have very little leverage, but as part of a buying group, there is power in numbers and you can get pricing that bigger restaurants and franchises have access to. I finally got to negotiate a 1% point over cost from my suppliers. I always ask for terms from all of them. 21 days is best, but if I can, I get 14 days.

- ❖ *For more helpful hints on maximizing your margins, check out the bonus action items (on [page #49](#)) (at the end of this chapter)!*

Reality #2: Trust your employees, but verify!

I had an employee who had been with me for 7 years. She was my second hire when I started the business. She had risen through the ranks and was now second in command and in charge of inventory. I thought she was a great employee and I also considered her family. I had never bought security cameras, but I saw a sale on Black Friday so decided to buy them and have them installed. It didn't take more than 1 day to see my trusted employee stealing over $750 worth of food right beneath my nose. It was a tough wake-up call, but one I will never forget. I keep that video surveillance clip on my desktop and look at it often so I remember that lesson. Since you can't be present all the time—and even if you were, you may not be able to detect the fraud going on—you have to create internal controls to help you.

Take away

Video surveillance and alarm equipment are great tools, but only if you use them and view them often. It may feel weird at first to think you have to "spy" on your employees, but don't learn the lesson the hard way like I did.

Another thing I find helpful is to do customer and employee surveys at least quarterly. This not only helps you understand where there is room for improvement in your own operation, but it may also point to an employee who may not be delivering the type of service you require.

Lastly, and most importantly, monitoring your KPI'S (key performance indicators) on a frequent basis (daily, weekly, monthly) is vital to understanding your business. If you consistently manage your KPI's, your team will focus on the right goals and you will see very quickly where you are missing the mark and can then determine why.

- ❖ *For more helpful hints on the KPIs you and your employees should be monitoring, check out the bonus action items (on page #50) (at the end of this chapter)!*

Reality #3: Customers expect more and more

Customers today demand great service, unbelievable products, and great value. And if they don't get it, they'll go on Yelp, Twitter, Facebook and more to tell everyone about it. And then there are the ones that don't say a word, but you lose them to your competitor. It's harder and harder to keep up with customer expectations, but it's not an option so you need a game plan on how you will do it.

Even five years ago, those of us with restaurants rarely heard a customer ask, "Does this contain _____?" Now, every restaurant is expected to cater to specific diets and allergies. It's become the norm. While only 2% of the population is truly allergic to wheat, more than 20% of Americans claim they do not eat wheat at all. And let's not get started with vegetarian, vegan, paleo and similar diets. A Disney World study found that 330,000 customers requested a specialty meal in their parks in 2009. Compare that to a whopping 675,000 people in 2014! That's double, in just 5 years!

The "free from" trend won't be going anywhere anytime soon. Customers will continue to expect you to cater to their needs. This means we need to find dishes within our menus that cater to these trends and advertise them as possible dining options.

The industry's biggest shift, however, is being propelled by Generations Y and Z and their search for convenience and simplicity. We'll touch more on this fascinating subject in Chapter 3, since it's an important trend within the industry and one of the main reasons I decided to write this book.

Take away

Understand who your customer is and what's important to them. The more you know about your ideal customer, the better you can tailor your offers to delight them. For instance, we know our core customers are busy professionals who want to eat healthy but don't have time to cook for themselves. For them, convenience is a key factor so delivering daily meals hassle-free to their work location is extremely important.

Track any online comments made about your company by setting up a Google Alert so whenever your company is mentioned, you get notified. This allows you to respond to online reviews (positive or negative) in a prompt matter. I recommend you answer with facts and in a non-confrontational way. It is always good for potential customers to see that you care and they can hear both sides of the story.

#3   Creating win-win programs such as loyalty programs, exclusive promotions, and pre-paid programs dare all great ways to build incentives for your customers to keep coming back to you. But don't take my word for it. Talk to your customers. Find out what they want.

Reality #4: Competition is expensive and very real

The restaurant industry is highly competitive with respect to price, value, service, location, and food quality. We already know customers are demanding and if there is another restaurant or food service business that is able to promote and deliver a higher degree of value, your business will suffer. McDonalds sells hamburgers for $1.00, yet a bell pepper can cost $2.50. So you know what? I don't try to compete with McDonalds.

The best way to beat the competition is to provide something better, faster or cheaper than they do. You can't do all of those things at once so you have to decide what your competitive advantage is and then work like hell to dominate.

Don't try to be all things to all people. It's better to do one thing really well than a dozen things mediocre.

Take away

Don't compete on price. It's tough to win loyal customers if they are always looking for a cheaper price. Make sure you have a strong competitive advantage and that it is clear and well communicated to your employees and customers so they understand your value in the market. Target customers that value what you offer and are willing to pay for it. If there isn't enough demand, change your model. Keep up to date with key trends. This is a great way to stay ahead of your competition and remain relevant to the marketplace as you will see in Chapter #4.

Reality #5: Running a restaurant may not be the ideal job you imagine

For those not yet in the industry, running a restaurant may seem like the ideal job. No office, lots of free food and an even larger salary. But those who have passionately pursued this dream have realized that it's not all food and drinks. Consider these harsh truths before you decide to enter the industry. You'll have to find ways to work around them like I did.

Restaurants don't take vacation days. The owner of a restaurant, especially a new one, will be required to work very long days and nights to ensure that everything is running smoothly. This includes weekends and most holidays, which are the busiest times for restaurants. If you're hoping to take your spouse out to dinner for Valentine's Day, you may want to consider taking them to your restaurant. If you do manage to get a day off, expect to be on the phone with your restaurant throughout the day. Gone but never forgotten.

In my case, I was able to shift this around by catering to the business crowd. When they're away, I'm away. I also created process and systems that would allow the business to run without me. I just came back from a 6 week vacation and my managers handled everything perfectly. But being away didn't mean that I wasn't unaware of what was going on with the business. Every manager sent me their KPIs and reports so I could make sure that everyone was doing their job.

Income will be unpredictable. Expect your salary to start at $0 and stay there for at least six months to a year, especially if you're opening your first restaurant. When business is slow, the first person who doesn't get paid will be you, the owner. If you ever envision expanding the business or putting more money into it, guess where that will come from: your paycheck.

You won't get company insurance. As a small business owner, you will have to purchase private insurance for you and your family. You may also want to account for retirement or your children's futures. You will not have an employer's 401K to utilize. Outside of your own benefits, you may also be required to subsidize your employees' insurance, which can impact your salary (or lack of one) even further.

You will initially be responsible for doing everything. The restaurant industry is so challenging because there are so many moving parts. As the owner, you must be prepared to take on every position at a moment's notice. You'll learn to be the owner of many hats very early on. Tomorrow you may be washing dishing and the following day you may be managing the bar. You will never know when you need an extra body until that body is not available to you. Then you'll be it.

You will never satisfy everyone. This was a tough one for me. Do you recall how many times you've said you wanted to own a restaurant? So has every person who's every visited Yelp. All those wannabe restauranteurs will look forward to telling you how to run and improve your restaurant. Even family, friends and employees will chime in. Every person you know or don't know (yet) will have an opinion and be adamant about your need to hear it. So before you get into the industry, realize that you will never satisfy everyone. Try not to let it get to you.

Take away

While this reality check paints a bleak picture of owning a restaurant, the truth is that it still does have many rewards. I just want to make sure you are aware of the realities we go through as restauranteurs. I was able to get through all of these issues and find success. Now I have my management team in charge of day-to-day operations, which frees up my time to pursue my other passion—helping foodpreneurs succeed and relinquish control.

Chapter 2 Summary

Reality #1: Margins are extremely tight

Key Learning: Focus on your volume first to grow, but margins need to be set and monitored! Make sure you have systems and processes in place so that as you grow, you don't grow at a loss.

Reality #2: Trust your employees, but verify!

Key Learning: You can't be present all the time so put systems in place to keep tabs on the key elements of your business. Video surveillance, customer and employee surveys, and constant measurement of KPIs are great ways to do this.

Reality # 3: Customers expect more and more

Key Learning: Understand your customers and what they are looking for. Don't discount your core product. Come up with ways to provide added value using pre-pay plans, loyalty cards and exclusive promos.

Reality #4: Competition is expensive and very real

Key Learning: Don't try to compete with everyone. Figure out your competitive advantage and then make sure you consistently do it well and deliver on your promise. Keep current on key trends so you stay relevant to your customers and a step ahead of the competition.

Reality #5: Running a restaurant may not be the ideal job you imagine

Key Learning: Every industry has its positives and negatives. Make sure you accept the reality of this one before you commit. If you've already been in this industry for some time, find a way to make changes that will allow you to work ON your restaurant instead of IN it.

Chapter 2 Bonus Action Items

This material expands on the ideas discussed in:
- ❖ Reality #1: Margins are extremely tight
- ❖ Reality #2: Trust your employees, but verify!

4 Ways to Maximize Your Margins Now

1. Ensure your menu is engineered to yield optimum gross margin

Push the meals that are your most profitable. Consider creating combination meals that offer seasonal fare in order to maximize your revenues. Take a second look: what you sell most might not be making you the most money.

2. Maximize buying leverage

A dollar saved in purchasing goes right to your bottom line, so try to purchase in bulk. You can boost your profit margin by one stop shopping to leverage your buying power.

3. Balance labor to meet demand

If you are overstaffing your restaurant, you are throwing profits out the window. Keep track of your high volume times and staff appropriately. Don't be afraid to cut wait staff on a slow night. They don't want to stand around anymore than you want them on the clock running up your costs. If you have to cut someone early, consider giving them a better shift on the next rotation to make up for it. Staffing to your needs will help keep you in the black.

4. **Get your customers to spend more money per transaction**

Consider adding side orders that consist of less expensive seasonal fare in order to boost your profit margins. Provide a drink menu and offer incentives with purchase, such as a free dessert. Pie is cheaper than liquor and it is surprising how much this can boost your per-ticket intake.

⭐ Are You On Top of Your Important KPIs? ⭐

A key performance indicator (KPI) is a business metric used to evaluate factors that are crucial to the success of an organization. KPIs are a vital navigation instruments that restaurant owners, managers, and eventually all employees should use to understand whether they are on course to success or not.

There's a business saying: 'if you can't measure it, you can't manage it!' Restaurant managers that use real, reliable figures can make better business decisions. KPIs can also identify where there are problems so corrective action can be taken quickly. If you are having success, you'll know to do more of what you're doing!

These restaurant KPIs are just a small selection of useful measurements you can monitor so you have the data to lead your restaurant in the right direction. KPI's should be in alignment with goals as well, so they may vary from restaurant to restaurant.

Even if you start with one KPI and build from there, you will be ahead of the game. When you start arming yourself with solid data and measure your management and employee performance, you will make better business decisions that lead to success.

1. **Number of customers**

    Reviewing how many customers your restaurant is serving on a daily, weekly or monthly basis is an important indicator you should be tracking and monitoring for increases or decreases.

2. **Average spend per customer**

    This figure is easy to work out using just two numbers: Total Sales divided by the Total Number of Customers. Tracking this can reveal opportunities for growth either by offering additional menu choices or training your staff to sell.

3. **Food costs**

    Identifying what you pay for every ingredient that goes into every menu item and then monitoring that for increases can help you determine if you need a new vendor source or a replacement item, or if you need to raise prices so you maintain appropriate margins.

4. **Gross profit**

    One way to measure gross profit can be to add up food purchases for the week and measure that against your food sales. Or you can break it down by product cost versus sales price.

5. Employee turnover

Employee turnover is the number of employees you must replace due to resignations and other separations during a given time period. Usually a month is a good time period. Employee turnover is an important way to measure both the effectiveness of your hiring processes and the overall management of your restaurant.

6. Revenue per employee

To calculate this KPI, take your company's revenue and divide it by your total employees. The numbers should be pulled from a corresponding duration of time—monthly, quarterly or annually. The revenue-per-employee ratio provides a broad indication of how expensive you restaurant is to run. It can be especially insightful when measuring efficiency.

7. New customers

Bringing in new business is important, which makes this another KPI every restaurant should measure. How many new customers you are acquiring on a monthly basis? How does that relate to your costs?

8. Customer retention

As a restaurant owner or manager, you know how important it is to retain customers. It is often cheaper to retain an existing customer then to acquire a new one. If you have a low customer retention rate, it is an indicator that they may not be happy with your product or service, or that they have replaced you with a competitor.

Chapter 2 Reflection

WHAT WILL YOU TAKE FROM THIS CHAPTER TO ADAPT TO YOUR PROFIT RECIPE?

_____

_____

_____

WHAT ARE THE TOP 3 ACTIONS YOU ARE GOING TO TAKE AS A RESULT OF THIS CHAPTER?

1. _____

   _____

2. _____

   _____

3. _____

   _____

CHAPTER 3: CALL A PSYCHIC

Where Is the Food Industry Headed?

In this chapter, I want to share some facts and research about where the restaurant business is headed, identify key consumer and industry trends, and provide some recommendations on how you can take advantage of this information to come up with more profit.

If you are just starting out, this research and data can help you identify your niche and competitive differentiation. If you are already established, this chapter will help you determine how to innovate and renovate. This is a very important chapter that I am particularly excited to share with you because it will help you not only understand what consumers want today, but also create a plan for how you are going to fulfill their desires: your own Profit Recipe!

Here are some facts and research to help identify top trends looking towards 2020.

Top Trend #1: Restaurant spending will continue to grow

It's a great market to be in, but you need to know what you are getting yourself into.

- According to data from the U.S. Census Bureau, the monthly sales at restaurants exceeded grocery store sales for the first time on record in December 2014 and continues to increase.

- Restaurant spending makes up 47% of the food dollar.

- Consumers spent $683.4 billion in restaurant industry sales in 2013.

- Food is the third highest expense in households after home and transportation.

- Americans eat out on average at least 5x a week, or 256 days a year.

- According to a National Restaurant Association survey conducted in May 2015, consumers benefiting from lower gas prices are reallocating their gas dollars towards eating out.

Take away

The food industry will continue to grow, but remember as we learned in Chapter #2, it will get tougher and tougher with low margins and high competition. It is important to focus on a niche, keep current on trends that set you apart from your competitors, and provide your clients with compelling reasons to stick with you. Focus on WHY they should choose you over the other options.

[handwritten: TASTE & FASTER!]

Top Trend #2: Consumers are looking for more convenience

- According to an NRA study, 70% of ALL restaurant foot traffic will be off premise by 2020. This is driven by the buying patterns of Gen Y and Z, who will become 80% of the work force in 2020. Examples of off-premise options include delivery, pickup, food trucks, curbside, etc.

- 75% of Americans said it is important to be able to order food online.

- 40-50% of office workers in urban areas eat at their desks on any given day.

- Consumers today, especially Gen Y and Millennials, make food decisions based on convenience.

- 55% of adults say they would order on a daily basis from restaurants if offered the choice and selection they desired.

- 50% of adults are not using delivery options as often as they would like.

- In 2014, 33% of adults said purchasing takeout food is essential to their lifestyle.

- More than half a billion venture capital dollars went into food delivery startups last year, more than triple the amount invested in the previous year.

Take away

Given the trend toward 70% of food traffic being off-premise by 2020, which is only a little over 5 years away, there is a huge opportunity to grow your market by adding an off-premise component to your business. Consider a delivery fleet, a food truck, curb-side pickup or any feature that provides more convenience to your customers. Remember what we learned in Chapter 1 and 2? We need to focus on our volume first to be relevant. What better way to grow volume than by riding the fastest growing trend and expanding your customer base using your same space and facilities?

I shifted Fit2Go's initial vision from a healthy café to a meal delivery service because as a Gen Y-er I saw the shift of consumers looking for convenience. That was 9 years ago! Today we sell more than 1000 meals per day and have revenues of more than 1.5M per year without a retail location. Imagine what you could do if you have a retail location AND you added more convenience with off-premise solutions! What type of volume could you add within your local market? What would that do to your margins? In Chapter #4 we will go more into how to take advantage of this trend based on your current model by digging deep into what your current customers are looking for.

❖ *For more helpful hints on convenience and appealing to Generations Y and Z, check out the bonus action items (on page #69) (at the end of this chapter)!*

Top Trend #3: Consumers want specialized food options that fit their changing lifestyles

- **It's about lifestyle.** According to a 2015 Mintel study, consumers are no longer worried about dieting—it's all about lifestyle. "Consumers are shunning restrictive fads in favor of a more holistic wellness approach."

- **"Free from" matters.** After years of consumer pressure, we are looking at the "healthification" of fast and fast-casual food. A recent survey found that 36% of consumers worried about "chemicals" in their food. In another survey, 40% of consumers reported that it's "very important" that foods contain all-natural ingredients that are free of GMOs and artificial flavors and colors.

- **Clean is the new green.** "The priority is transparency. Consumers want to know more about ingredients, products and the companies that make and sell them...Currently, 80% of consumers look for nutritional claims (i.e. vitamins, fiber) when buying food, while over one third (38%) look for products that are all natural. Food origin is also quickly becoming a purchase factor, with 35% of consumers seeking products that carry a local claim." *A.T. Kearney*

- **Knowledge is power.** According to ConsumerReports.org, 46% of clients are bothered when restaurant staff and servers do not know the ingredients in a certain dish or how it was prepared.

- **Healthier options.** 64% of respondents ranked the availability of healthy menu options as important in choosing where to dine.

- **Gluten-free diets dominate.** According to Newswire, "66% of experts believe gluten-free or wheat-free diets will continue to be trendy ... consumers believe that eliminating foods with certain ingredients will help them lose weight or be healthier."

- In the same study, dieticians also noted that we will see **'clean eating'** as well as the **Paleo diet** as popular eating trends.

- **"Low-fat" fizzles.** "While low-carb remains strong, low-fat gets weaker. For another consecutive year, the overwhelming majority of dieticians predict that the low-fat diet will fall flat in 2015, with only 4% naming it as a popular eating trend among consumers.

- **The risc of vegetarian and its variations.** Meat-free diets have become "an aspirational lifestyle choice," says the JWT agency. These include ovo-vegetarian, pecatarian, vegan, vegetarian, etc. The Vegetarian Resource Group found that 30-40% of American adults regularly eat vegetarian meals, but only 4-5% of adults are full-time vegetarians and only 1-2.5% are full-time vegans.

Take away

I adapted these trends into my model by offering portion control, fresh healthy offerings, daily delivery, and a diet component. I constantly stay up to date on new lifestyle trends and adapt our offerings based on them. For instance, in the last 3 years the "Paleo" diet became a big growth trend in our area due to the rise of CrossFit. I already had the menu items and the ingredients to cater to that need, so it was just a matter of making it known we offered this. Had I not done that, I would have lost current and future business to the competition.

You could use your same menu, or tweak or add new dishes that position your restaurant as a lifestyle brand so your customers order more from you. By lifestyle brand, I mean a place where your customers would order from more than 3 times a week. The key is to understand who your customer is and what niche you can cater to. Think about how you are going to become part of their life so they want to order from you every day or multiple times a week. It may be that you already have the menu items, but you've never packaged it as a lifestyle brand and service to order from consistently. Or maybe you need to come up with new menu items that your customers want to order from every day of the week. You can get creative here and attract a new audience as well. Most probably, you already have the customers, and you just need to determine what they want.

Gluten-free, paleo, vegetarian, locally produced meats and produce...I'm not suggesting that you try to be all things to all people or jump on every new health trend. But I am suggesting that you pay attention to what's important to your customers and find ways to incorporate them into your menu. So survey your customers, talk to them, test things. Find out what they want. Don't think that because you have a thriving restaurant clientele today that they will be here tomorrow. Give them a reason to keep coming back.

I believe every restaurant can take advantage of this powerful trend, no matter what your specialty is. If you are an Italian restaurant, can you promote a Mediterranean diet? If you are a Hindu restaurant, can you promote a vegetarian diet? Find out if there is a common theme that your customers appreciate: Kosher, Vegetarian, Organic, Fresh, Home-made, Comfort food... Can you create a weekly offering to cater to their needs? Of course you can. You just need to do it!

There is a quote by George Bernard Shaw that says, "There is no sincerer love than the love of food." Being in the restaurant business gives you a place in your customer's heart that few other businesses can find. Taking care of them by introducing them to new trends or adapting to things that are important to them will ensure you keep the love alive.

Top Trend #4: Restaurants must leverage technology to reach and serve customers

- 51% of recently surveyed consumers said they consider it important for restaurants to integrate technology into their ordering capabilities.

- Technology related to ordering, coupons or special offers sent via email and text messaging have some of the highest usage rates in the industry, as 58% of survey respondents said they use such gadgets at least once a month.

- Restaurants need to use technology to have better access to their data, save time, deal with issues in real-time, be consistent with data collection, and be more eco-friendly.

- 62% of customers are less likely to go to a particular restaurant if they cannot easily read the menu on their mobile device. This means you could be losing more than half of your potential customers if your website is not up to date!

Take away

Since I focused my core market on health conscious professionals, I knew I had to add a simple online ordering process to the platform.

It is important to have systems and software that can help you with all your processes, make all your follow-ups automatically, and skim down your labor costs wherever you can. Look at things like menu management, customer management, order and delivery management and marketing management. Above all, don't replace work for work. Use software that optimizes your processes, saves you money by reducing labor costs, and improves your performance. The capital required to build your own software can quickly add up, so consider purchasing software as a service package from a vendor (Such as Fit2go DS).

Top Trend #5: Political and social trends will also influence the restaurant industry

1. **The possible end of franchising as we know it**

The National Labor Relations Board has declared that restaurant franchisors can be held accountable for the labor practices and policies of its franchisees. This means franchisors must control business fundamentals including shift scheduling across the tens of thousands, which is not an easy task. Without proper regulation, lawsuits will come flooding in, so we may see big brands franchising less and focusing more on corporate development instead. Another factor playing into this is the outrageous royalty fees Franchisors charge their Franchisees. Since they are based on revenue, it is difficult for the franchisee to find a decent profit with today's environment.

2. Unions gain momentum

This one goes along with the possible end of franchising, as the ruling was also a go-ahead for unions to bring complaints against franchisees. But that wasn't the only reason for unions' new momentum. We also saw an increase in nationwide job demonstrations and walkouts as well as considerable media coverage concerning wages.

3. Big changes in the minimum wage and how it's raised

As mentioned above, we've seen big changes concerning minimum wage in the restaurant industry. In just one day, six different states approved a minimum wage increase through votes as opposed to legislatures. Ballots are now the preferred means for unions to push for desired changes. A new model in which minimum wages are indexed to inflation has been introduced, which means that future increases in minimum wage rates will occur automatically.

4. Menu labeling required for ready-to-eat food

The FDA revealed the particulars of the menu-labeling requirements in the Affordable Care Act. One major point for restaurants (as well as convenience stores and supermarkets) is that they must abide by menu-labeling rules for ready-to-eat foods.

5. Tipping undergoes a revolution

With an increased enforcement of tipping laws that have been around for decades, we've seen a huge change in the way tipping in restaurants is viewed. While tipping violations may not seem like a big deal, the penalties can quickly pile up. Many operators have begun experimenting with service charges in response to an increase in federal investigations and class-action suits concerning conventions such as tip pooling and tip sharing.

Chapter 3 Summary

Imagine combining all the highest growing trends as I did with Fit2Go and adding it to your business model! Create a lifestyle brand that caters to a specific niche, and add the convenience of delivering it to your customers several times a week. Picture what it could do for your profit margin! You already have the kitchen, your staff, and your menu. You are just adding variable costs to your model. All your gross profit would go straight to your bottom line! There is a huge opportunity for restaurants that start thinking this way and stay relevant to their clients. Plus, you can start making higher profits very easily.

Top Trend #1: Restaurant spending will continue to increase

Key Learning: It's a big competitive market, so in order to stand out and get noticed, it is important to identify your niche and focus on important trends that set you apart and provide your clients with compelling reasons to stick with you.

Top Trend 2: Your consumers are looking for more convenience

Key Learning: It is predicted that by 2020, 70% of food traffic will be off-premise. This creates a huge opportunity to grow your market and revenue by adding a delivery component to your business.

Top Trend #3: Consumers want options that fit their lifestyles

Key Learning: Keep current on what your customers want, i.e. healthier choices, gluten free, vegetarian, etc. Figure out how to become an important, yet convenient, part of their life so they want to order from you every day or multiple times a week. Become a lifestyle brand.

Top Trend #4: Restaurants must leverage technology to reach and serve customers

Key Learning: It is important to have systems and software that can help you with your critical processes such as menu management, customer management, order management and marketing management to relieve your payroll and streamline your results.

Top Trend #5: Political and social trends will also influence the restaurant industry

Key Learning: We always need to be on top of current news and external factors that could change the way we do business. It is important to be ready for any case scenario.

Chapter 3 Bonus Action Items

This bonus material expands on the ideas discussed in:
- ❖ Trend #2: Consumers are looking for more convenience

How Generations Y and Z Are Shifting the Industry

You want your restaurant to do well, and that means you need to be marketing to millennials. One of the demographics that's starting to spend more time and money in restaurants are Generations Y and Z. These are the people who were born in 1979 or after. By 2020 they will account for 80% of the workforce.

Of course, you have to realize that this generation is very different from the generations who came before. They are the millennial generation; they grew up when the Internet was already a thing. They're able to text faster than most people can type, and they are constantly taking photos and making videos. They grew up with touch screen devices, which have become an integral part of their lives—even an extension of their minds. So what does this mean for your restaurant?

1. They want convenience

As we said previously, and the most daunting data point of all... 70% of ALL restaurant foot traffic will be off premise by 2020! This is a trend you can't ignore. If you want to have a place in your current and future customers' lifestyle, make sure you offer convenient options. For instance, if you don't currently offer a delivery or pick-up option, consider it. You could even consider creating a food truck version of your restaurant with a whittled-down menu that you can take to the areas where your customers tend to congregate, or where you want to entice new customers.

2. They want technology

Think about how this generation will access information about your restaurant—through the internet. This means you need to have a high quality, modern, device responsive website that shows off your menu, even when the site is viewed from a mobile device. Your site also needs to load quickly and the menu needs to be accessible and simple. If it's too complex or too slow, they will likely just find somewhere it's easier to figure out what they want to eat.

3. They need digital menus

Some restaurants have mobile apps that allow customers to place orders through their phone after they've been seated, which eliminates the need for a server to take their order. While this does cut down on the human experience that dining out typically offers, that's what many in this generation are coming to expect. In addition to having an app, some restaurants actually have tablets on their tables that customers use to order, which means there is no interaction with your servers until their drinks and food are delivered.

4. They want free Wi-Fi

Even though it would have been considered bad manners to keep your face buried in a screen at the restaurant even just a few years ago, today it is the norm. People don't want to waste their data plan, so make sure that you offer wireless internet they can access. If they have a choice between a restaurant that offers this and one that doesn't, they will choose the one with Wi-Fi almost every time.

Chapter 3 Reflection

WHAT WILL YOU TAKE FROM THIS CHAPTER TO ADAPT TO YOUR PROFIT RECIPE?

_____

_____

_____

WHAT ARE THE TOP 3 ACTIONS YOU ARE GOING TO TAKE AS A RESULT OF THIS CHAPTER?

1. _____

    _____

2. _____

    _____

3. _____

    _____

MUST ALIGN OUR BIZ THIS WAY!

Chapter 4: The Profit Recipe

How to Boost Your Margins Using the Food Industry's Top Trends

    I am hoping by this point you see the value in building a lifestyle component as part of your offering in order to increase the number of times your customers order from you and create a recurring business model. Remember, by lifestyle brand, I mean an option where your customers would order from more than 3 times per week.

Now imagine adding a delivery component to it... Picture what it could do for your profit margin! You already have the kitchen, your staff, and your menu. You are just adding variable costs to your model. All your gross profit would go straight to your bottom line!

There is a huge opportunity for restaurants that start thinking this way and stay relevant to their clients. Plus you can start making higher profits very easily.

In this chapter, I am going to provide the checklists and processes to help you get there. Utilizing these tools are great best practices for any restaurant, but especially when you are working toward securing your position as a successful lifestyle brand in the hearts and minds of your customers - current and new. Before we go any further I want to highlight a couple ground rules:

1. Think of the delivery component as an extension of your business. DON'T STOP what you are currently doing that works for you.

2. Figure out the needs of your customers that you are not presently providing so you don't cannibalize your current business, although cannibalization can be good if the net effect is greater as a result. For

example, adding curbside delivery may initially take away from your sit-in diners, but if they now frequent your establishment two or three times a week versus one or two times a month, it's well worth it.

3. Start your delivery programs slowly, area by area, so you can test out and refine your processes.

Okay, with these insights in mind, let's get back to the checklists and processes you need to go through. These checklists are focused on four key areas. As you go through each checklist, it will become clear where you need to place your focus.

In my experience, it became overwhelming to manage all these checklists manually, so I used Fit2Go DS and it transformed my business. It allowed me to create and manage my systems and processes which resulted in my company becoming a successful, scalable, growth-oriented business. Regardless of whether you choose to keep track of it manually or use Fit2Go DS to do it for you, here are the 4 key areas you need to develop control processes for in your lifestyle brand restaurant:

1. Customer Management
2. Menu Management
3. Order and Delivery Management
4. Marketing Management

CUSTOMER MANAGEMENT
Know your market and carve out your niche

Strategic Alignment Checklist
- Does your restaurant have a mission statement, vision and values?
- Are you using your mission, vision and values to drive your business?
- How do you want your customers to perceive your brand (playful, formal, gourmet, simple, comfort)?
- Do you deliver your brand promise in everything you do? How do you test and measure that?

Current Customer Checklist
- Identify your current customers.
- Describe them in detail (their likes, dislikes, pains, what they look for).
- Create a database of their information.
- Determine any needs and wants they have that you aren't currently providing.
- Routinely survey them to ensure you understand what they need.

- Identify new customers you can target by adding a lifestyle delivery component.

Competitive Differentiation and Landscape Checklist

- Identify any competition vying for the same customer.
- Routinely sample and visit your competition.
- Determine what you can provide that will make your restaurant unique.
- Identify unique attributes set you apart from your competitors.
- Provide new offerings that attract new customers.
- Ask your customers to rank you on the following: food, service, convenience, atmosphere, location, choices, etc.

Customer Retention Checklist

- List offerings you can provide that will create recurring business.
- Create materials and a plan to communicate with your customers on a consistent basis.
- Determine a schedule to routinely send them promotions and reminders.
- Send out periodic surveys to see how you are doing and what they may want more of.

- Create loyalty programs to reward your best customers.
- Monitor review sites and address both positive and negative comments.

Take away

Know your customers and find out what's important to them. They may not know exactly what they want, but if you learn about their lifestyle, their habits and their needs, you can come up with ways to provide them with choices that make their life better, more convenient and enjoyable. It's so important to have processes in place to consistently communicate with them. Your customers and a compelling "why you exist" are the foundation for your success.

Remember, your customers don't want to hear about your policies and procedures. They want satisfaction. Client concerns don't always have to end badly. Connecting with them using social media allows you to parlay a bad review into an opportunity to engage with your clients and market your business at the same time.

- ❖ *For more helpful tips on ways turning bad reviews into more sales go to page 87 (at the end of this chapter!)*

MENU MANAGEMENT
Lifestyle Menu Settings Checklist

- Determine who your target customers are for your menu.
- Develop a menu using as many ingredients that you are already using in existing dishes.
- Provide an unexpected twist with you menu items that delights the customer.
- Determine if your customers are able to make changes to your menu, or if it is a fixed menu.
- Determine how many dishes will compose a menu and standardize all menus so it is simple to classify.
- Make sure the items on the menu will travel well.
- Determine if any special packaging is needed.
- Think about whether or not the items need to be eaten right away or can easily be reheated.
- If they can be easily reheated, figure out if you will need special containers that can go in microwave.
- Make sure you separate cold items from hot items.
- Make sure you routinely add samples of other menu items you want your customers to sample for future purchases or to get feedback about new menu items.

Lifestyle Recipe Set-Up Checklist

- Create a list of every ingredient you use for all your menu items.
- Create a standardized recipe for every dish. Every item should be measured and controlled up to the amount of salt and pepper (Yes, this may make your chef mad but it's the only way you can control costs as well as quality on a consistent basis).
- Determine costs per portion.
- Make sure you have all the nutritional information for each dish.
- Highlight any allergy warnings for each recipe.
- Determine if you will have alternate menus for people allergic to your menu of the day.
- Put triggers in your system to add/change menu items to take advantage of seasons/local savings.

Purchasing Checklist

- Create a weekly shopping list with all the ingredients you need.
- Get quotes from 3 different vendors each time you purchase. Be certain your quotes are comparing the exact same items.
- Make sure you have Net 21 or 14 terms with each of your vendors. (Note: With Fit2Go Delivery System Software (FDS), I receive my shopping list and

quote each week with all my ingredients from each vendor so I can choose the lowest costs.)
- Create a process to control inventory on what goes in and out of each section of your kitchen.
- Have different people cross-check inventory/purchasing and receiving in order to minimize theft.
- Join a purchasing group.

Take away

In order to develop a lifestyle brand and delivery system, you do not have to reinvent the wheel with your menu. Develop your menu so it builds on top of your current sales by tweaking a few things, and leverage your core strengths. Design a program that your customers will want 3 - 5 times a week and that will create a recurring purchasing model for your business. Make sure that once the customer receives their order, they have a great experience consuming it.

- ❖ *For more helpful tips on ways you can cut costs associated with your menu, negotiate with vendors for the best prices and use industry trends to keep things fresh, check out the bonus material (on page 91 & 93) (at the end of this chapter)!*

ORDER & DELIVERY MANAGEMENT
Off-Premise Model Checklist

- Determine if you are going to add an off-premise model like delivery, takeout, curbside pickup and/or food trucks.
- Have a simple and convenient online ordering process for your clients.
- Determine cap time for customers to order: same day, same week, Friday before, etc.
- Make sure your order process captures important information for reporting and future marketing.
- Determine what systems you will use for payment. Credit Card is always better to collect your fees upfront, but if your market requires cash/checks, have a clear process in place during delivery.
- Determine what your minimum allowed order is ($X, 1 meal, 1 day, 1 week, 1 month, etc.).
- Determine whether or not you will have an automatic renewal model so customers don't have to order on a weekly/monthly basis, and if so, is it required for all customers?

Order Tracking Checklist

- Have a process to print all labels for the day: both customer labels and dish labels.
- Have an organized way of seeing all orders for the day and what each customer ordered (and if they need any dish changed due to allergies/dislikes).

Delivery Checklist

- Evaluate whether you should use a 3rd party versus in-house delivery fleet.
- If you choose in-house fleet, determine if you will classify them as employees or 1099 contracted drivers.
- Evaluate the advantages of using routes versus back/forth versus on-demand delivery providers versus pick up locations.
- Find a routing system that helps you design the optimal route.
- Determine what type of signage will be used for vehicles that deliver to your customers.
- Determine if you will provide your drivers with uniforms.
- Determine if your delivery process is going to be retail versus wholesale oriented. i.e. deliver directly

to customers at each address or deliver to pickup locations/distributors; or both.

Take away

Track your revenue and costs from deliveries as separate line items on your sales report so you can monitor how much profit you're earning from this service. Evaluate all your costs to develop efficiencies in your ordering and delivery processes to save costs. When you add delivery service to your restaurant business, you've added a new revenue source but also a new level of complexity to manage. The right technology will help you keep control of your delivery operation – and make it more profitable. Delivery can make up a profitable portion of your business if you have the right tools in place.

- ❖ *For more helpful hints on revving up sales with a user-friendly ordering system and why you should add a delivery component to your business (as well as the questions to ask before you do)*, **check out the bonus material (on pages 95, 97, 100, 102) (at the end of this chapter)!**

MARKETING MANAGEMENT

Track and Measure Checklist

- Determine your costs to acquire a new customer.
- Identify your retention index.
- Develop ways to constantly improve retention.
- Track promotions to determine if they are successful.
- Track buying patterns to determine triggers and seasonality to consider.
- Create a way to collect emails to add to your database that you can market to. Make sure to put them in the right category so you communicate with customers differently than prospects.
- Create a system to send recurring follow up emails.
- Develop a newsletter to send out on a consistent basis.
- Use social media to engage with your audience.
- Plan quarterly surveys.

Competitive Advantage Checklist

- Create "added value" items that result in increased spending.
- Develop a system to promote specials with same-day efficiency.
- Consistently provide benefits that your competitor can't offer.
- Create programs to generate business during slow periods.
- Encourage customers to share reviews and recommendations.
- Test promotional offers and new menu items.

Take away

The best promotion starts with providing a high quality product that your customers value, and consistently delivering it with excellent service. Nothing will kill a bad product faster than great promotion, so it always starts with your product and service. Use your current network and database to communicate your new offerings. Make sure you include fliers and coupons to all your customers and deliveries, plus mention your new services as often as you can and wherever you can.

We used our food as our best marketing tool when we first started, and we routinely gave away free lunches so people could experience our meals for themselves. We always provided them with an extra incentive to order after that so we could convert as many customers as possible. That worked really well for us. We also left fliers on cars of businesses we wanted to target and in as many lobbies as we could get into.

- ❖ *For more helpful hints on <u>building your marketing plan</u>, <u>using social media</u>, how <u>content marketing</u> can help cultivate customer relationships and more, check out the bonus material (on pages 107, 111 & 114) (at the end of this chapter)!*

Chapter 4 Summary

As you go through these checklists, you may start to feel overwhelmed and anxious as you realize how many things you need systems or processes for. My goal here isn't to stress you out, it's to help educate you on what you need to pay attention to in order to build and grow a successful lifestyle delivery business.

When I first started my business, I was involved in everything! Like I said in Chapter 1, I was customer service, operations, delivery man plus the CEO. If I had kept going like that, I probably wouldn't be around today either because I would have burnt out or my business wouldn't have been able to survive. It was only by taking the time to develop all the right systems and processes that I was able to grow without killing myself.

My company continues to grow every year, and more importantly, my team and I are working smarter. By having access to all our KPIs, we can invest our time in figuring out how to improve things, as well as continuously look out to the future to ensure we stay in sync with our customers. Whether you decide to use excel spreadsheets to do this for your restaurant or license Fit2Go DS, the fact is it needs to be done in order to grow your business. You cannot manage what you cannot measure, and if you aren't managing your business, you will end up like so many other hopeful restaurateurs that couldn't make it.

Customer Management

Key Learning: Know your customers and find out what's important to them. You can come up with ways to provide them with choices that make their life better, more convenient and enjoyable.

Menu Management

Key Learning: You don't have to reinvent the wheel with your menu to develop a lifestyle brand. This is easily done by tweaking a few things in your menu, and leveraging your core strengths. Design a program that your customers will want 3-5 times a week and that will create a recurring purchasing model for your business.

Order and Delivery Management

Key Learning: Evaluate all your costs to develop efficiencies in your ordering and delivery processes in order to save costs. When you add a delivery service to your restaurant business, you've added a new revenue source but also a new level of complexity to manage. The right technology will help you keep control of your delivery operation – and make it more profitable.

Marketing Management

Key Learning: The best promotion starts with providing a high quality product that your customers value, and consistently delivering it with excellent service. If you don't track your marketing efforts, it is difficult to determine if they have a good return on investment.

Chapter 4 Bonus Action Items
This bonus material expands on the ideas discussed in:

- ❖ Customer management
- ❖ Menu management
- ❖ Order and deliver management
- ❖ Marketing management

How You Can Turn Problems Into Profits

Whether you own, manage or operate a restaurant, social media may be the key to expanding your business and increasing your brand reputation. An excellent review on Yelp or Opentable isn't just free publicity, often times it leads to increased profit. Many restaurateurs encourage customers to rate their establishments on these review sites. Facebook reviews are now even a thing, so you can combine your reviews with your social media engagement!

Just don't assume that because you encourage reviews they'll always be favorable. Some restaurateurs are reticent to take advantage of everything that social media has to offer for fear that a bad review will take away more business than a good one can generate. Don't be afraid of negative reviews. Think of a negative review as an opportunity to make a contact with a customer and affect positive change within your business. How you handle customer disputes will determine whether they return to your restaurant in the future.

Using social media to effectively handle customer disputes can lead to more business and happier customers. No matter what the situation, you have the technology to turn it around. Complaints may range from food and service problems to your customers' mood. Whatever the problem, it's important to solve the dispute in a professional way. These quick and easy tips will help you turn problems into profit in no time.

1. Monitor your online presence

Monitoring your online presence is imperative in today's hyper-electronic culture. Social media is the key to building your business and expanding your brand. Part of this is protecting your brand and its reputation, so make sure you have someone monitoring your reviews and responding quickly and positively.

Never respond negatively, no matter how horrible the review may seem. Clearly the customer lodging the complaint has access to the internet and knows how to use it. Rather than justifying the complaint, validate it, even though it may be unwarranted. Yelp and Opentable attract traffic to your business; by handling a poor review in a positive way, you'll have the opportunity to turn that customer's experience around. You'll also mitigate its effect on other potential customers by showing that you care.

2. Listen carefully

The best way to do this online is to reply to the customer and ask them to elaborate on their concerns. Let them know you care that they had a poor experience in your establishment and reiterate how eager you are to make it right. Once you have a complete grasp on their concern, offer them the solution. Remember, business is business and the complaint isn't a personal attack. Resist becoming defensive at all costs. All they want is a solution. When you reply, ensure that you validate their concerns. Sometimes that is all they are seeking. As much as possible, try to take the discussion offline. Offer them other ways to get in touch so that the whole process isn't out there for everyone to see. Never let it devolve into an argument.

3. The customer is always right

Believe it or not, the old adage isn't that far off the mark. The successful restaurateur knows that even though the customer may be wrong, they are still the backbone of their business. Use the tools that social media provides to offer them a solution. Ask them to give you another try and send them a certificate to use the next time they visit. Ask them to come at a time when you will be there so that you can ensure that their experience is all that it can be.

4. Empathize

Imagine being in your customer's shoes. How would you feel? What solution would satisfy you in a similar situation? If you find that you are at a loss, ask the customer directly what solution they would suggest. Meet them half way if you are unable to grant their request.

5. Solve the problem quickly and own the mistake

This is often the most difficult to do. Owning a mistake you may not believe is yours is a challenge, but you will find that it almost immediately curtails the customer's frustration and opens the door to a resolution. Be transparent and let them know when the problem will be fixed. Make sure that you solve the dispute expeditiously and avoid having anyone else handle online/social media that is not management. Bottom line: customers need to feel their issue was handled correctly.

6. To comp or not to comp?

Sometimes a freebie is the way to go. While not the most cost effective in the short term, the profit it leads to in the long term may be worth it. Sometimes small comps are effective in appeasing an angry patron. Here are a few you can provide quickly and easily via an e-certificate or downloadable coupon that always rouse interest in a return visit:

- Free drinks
- Free dessert
- A discount (or free comp) on their meal
- Gift certificate for a future visit

Remember, your customers don't want to hear about your policies and procedures. They want satisfaction. Client concerns don't always have to end badly. Connecting with them using social media allows you to parlay a bad review into an opportunity to engage with your clients and market your business at the same time.

How to Negotiate With Food Vendors

Alongside labor, food costs are going to be one of your biggest expenses. That's why it's important to track and measure your margins to ensure your business is profitable. It's possible for a restaurant to be well-loved and unprofitable. If you've never owned a restaurant or food business, you may not know how to negotiate with your food vendors for the best prices, but these 5 tips will help:

1. Work with more than one

Working with only one vendor is one of the biggest mistakes restaurant owners make—myself included. When you only have one food source, you aren't able to compare pricing between vendors. By working with more than one vendor, you have options and can compare prices so that you can make sure you're not over-paying.

2. Create a food cost analysis

If you want to make sure that you're getting the best prices from vendors, you need to first understand how much each meal and portion costs. You need to know exactly what ingredients are needed and how much of them you'll need. Food costs can change dramatically from week to week, so it's a good idea to have a general knowledge of average prices and seasonality. Your average food costs should be between 28–32% percent of the overall expenses.

3. Use a bidding system

While it can be useful to give one vendor the majority of your purchase (as long as they agree to a fixed cost-plus model), you need to make sure that you are checking these prices against other vendors weekly. A bidding system allows you to create a competitive environment that will benefit your business. This is where using Fit2Go DS helps. This platform helps track and measure data so you can make better management decisions.

4. Join a restaurant buying group

Joining a restaurant buying group will allow you to leverage the purchasing power of multiple restaurants in order to obtain discounts from vendors due to the collective buying power of the members. There is power in numbers. Joining a buying group can help get you the pricing that franchises and bigger restaurants have access to.

5. Don't stop checking costs

Costs change frequently so you need to be vigilant about checking them often. The better informed you are about the costs of ingredients, the easier it will be for you to make smarter decisions about buying.

Negotiation is a skill, but it is one that can be learned and improved upon. By using these 5 tips you can ensure that you are doing all you can to keep your food costs low while aiming for higher profits.

Keep Your Menu Fresh by Staying Ahead of Trends

Staying on top of current food trends is one of the best ways to keep your menu fresh in terms of both food and variety. This goes along with choosing seasonal food items, but you also need to make sure that you're giving your customers what they want. With more and more people looking for healthier items or wanting vegan or gluten free options, you need to make sure that you're on top of current trends so that you offer what your customers are looking for.

1. Source locally

Local farm-to-food and sea-to-food restaurants are becoming increasingly popular, and it's an easy way to make sure that the food you're getting is fresh and local. If you're getting it straight from the farm, you are getting items in season that will taste fresh and delicious. Plus it's a great way to give back to the community (which is also something you can use in your marketing).

2. Change your menu seasonally

I've mentioned this before, but changing your menu seasonally not only lets you make sure that you're not including mango in a dish when mangoes aren't at their best, but also that you're keeping your variety fresh and new to keep customers coming back and excited to try new things. You can have a static menu that is always available, but having a special menu that changes based on seasonality can really bring your restaurant to the next level. People may look forward to one seasonal dish you serve all year—and visit often to get their fill of it before it's gone.

3. Get changeable menu boards

Some printed menus or static menu boards can be hard and costly to change. Don't let the way you communicate your menu interfere with being able to keep it fresh and relevant. Great options are having a blackboard where you can write the specials or seasonal menu items, inserts that can easily slip in your current menu cover or new digital options than can be updated by computer.

4. Go out and eat

Don't get so busy with your own restaurant that you don't go out and experience what other restaurants and food businesses are doing in your own neighborhood and beyond. Try all types of restaurants on a frequent basis to see what the competition is doing and get inspired. Don't just frequent restaurants in your space though. Try food trucks, ethnic food, specialty shops and think about how you can incorporate new flavors into existing dishes or add new dishes.

5. Find reputable food sources

In order to keep your menu fresh, and make sure that you don't overextend your budget, you want to make sure you find reputable and price-friendly food sources. Plus, your vendors can be a great resource for up and coming ingredients you may want to add to new menu items.

Fit2Go DS can help you create a cost analysis that allows you to determine the cost of your ingredients so you can create a bidding system with vendors to ensure you are getting the best price possible. Food costs can change dramatically from week to week, so this helps you get the best price each week.

5 Reasons to Add a Delivery Component Soon

If you own or manage a restaurant, you've probably had people asking you about delivery and considered adding it to your business, but you may have wondered if it's worth it. Considering that by 2020, 70% of ALL restaurant foot traffic will be off premise, deliver will be worth it—here's why:

1. **People want delivery**

    The honest truth is that if someone wants to eat at home, they are going to either cook themselves or get delivery, and very few things will change their minds. If you want a meal at home, you're going to eat a meal at home even if your favorite restaurant doesn't deliver. 50% of adults are not using delivery options as often as they would like and 55% of adults say they would order on a daily basis from restaurants if offered the choice and selection they desired. Adding a delivery component to your business can help you reach that market.

2. **It shows confidence that you can handle major exposure**

    Having a delivery component in your restaurant is definitely more work, but it looks good to your customers. Not only does it offer them an added level of convenience, it also shows that you are confident enough in the way your business is run that you know you can handle the added delivery component.

3. Your competitors are doing it

The bottom line is that if you don't deliver, your potential customers are going to get it from a competitor that does. We no longer live in an age where only a handful of restaurants deliver. Your customer may love your restaurant, but that doesn't always mean they are going to get up and go there. What it does mean is that they may choose to place a delivery order with you over someone else—but only if you offer delivery.

4. It's a win-win for everyone

You open your door to more business, and consequently more revenue, and your customers get more convenience. The situation is a win-win for everyone, and if you don't offer a delivery option, you could be losing out on a huge opportunity to your competitors.

Remember, while implementing a delivery component into your restaurant can be the final thing that pushes you to the success you've always wanted, you need to have the proper processes in place in order to do it successfully.

7 Questions to Ask Before Implementing Delivery

We've raved about why it's so important to add a delivery component to your restaurant business, but you need to remember that with adding a delivery component comes more complexity—and with more complexity comes more important decisions you need to make. To make the process easier for you and to help you determine the right course of action for your business, we've compiled a delivery checklist questionnaire to ask yourself.

1. **Should you use a third party or an in-house delivery fleet?**

    The answer depends on how much time you have to put into your delivery plan, as well as the demand your food business has for delivery. If you don't have the time or demand for delivery, it may make sense to use a third party. Alternatively, if your delivery orders are going through the roof, it may make sense to hire a dedicated delivery driver and handle it in house.

2. **If you choose to use an in-house fleet, will you classify them as employees or 1099 contracted drivers?**

    This will often depend on how high your demand for delivery is. If you have multiple delivery orders each hour, you will likely want a full-time employee by your side. If you only receive a few per day, it may make more sense for you to simply contract drivers that will be on-call for certain period of the day.

3. What's the best way to get food from your restaurant to your customers?

Does it make more sense to use routes, which is best for companies like Fit2Go that deliver daily food to customers); back and forth delivery, which is good for companies that want to dispatch an employee when a delivery order comes because they don't necessarily have a high demand for delivery; on-demand delivery providers, which are useful for restaurants that don't receive many delivery orders and thus don't need a dedicated delivery driver in the restaurant at all times; or pick-up locations, which often work well for companies that deliver mass quantities of food in a specific area? This will depend on your restaurant and what you want to achieve with the delivery side of your business.

4. How will you design the optimal route?

If you choose to use routes to get your food to your customer, how will you find the optimal route? This is a question where technology really comes into play. While every area is different, there are routing systems that can design the optimal route for you.

5. What type of signage are you going to use for delivery vehicles?

This often depends on whether you are using a third party or in-house delivery fleet. Using a 3rd party may not even give you this option, but you need to determine whether or not you want some sort of signage on delivery vehicles. Do you have company delivery vehicles or do employees use their own car? If you have a company delivery vehicle, you should definitely have signage on it. Vehicle wraps, or even partial wraps, can be extremely effective. If employees are using their own car, you may want to think about removable signage that they can take off after hours.

6. Will you provide your drivers with uniforms?

This also often depends on whether you are using a third party or an in-house delivery fleet, but how recognizable do you want your drivers to be? If you have a restaurant that delivers all the time (think pizza places like Domino's or Papa John's), it probably makes sense to provide your drivers with uniforms. If you have only just started delivering to customers and have a just a few deliveries a day, it may not be the best time to think about uniforms yet—especially if the employees working in your restaurant don't even wear a uniform.

7. **Are you going to deliver directly to your customers at each address or deliver to certain pickup locations or distributors? Retail or Wholesale? Or will you do both?**

This one really depends on the type of business you offer. If you're a single restaurant that is adding an in-house delivery component, it makes more sense for you to deliver directly to your customers (as oftentimes the main reason for ordering delivery to your house is so that you don't have to go anywhere). Alternatively, if you're in a situation where you have consistent deliveries going out at certain times for all of your customers in one area (think of a food delivery service that sends packages to customers once per week), it may make more sense for you to have a pick-up window with specific times for your customers to come to. If your customers are willing to come once a week to a pick-up location, it's much easier for you than it is to deliver to them all individually.

When you add delivery service to your restaurant business, you've added a new revenue source but also a new level of complexity to manage. The right technology and strategy will help you keep control of your delivery operation and make it more profitable.

4 Advantages of an Online Ordering System

1. Expanded reach

The advantages of an online ordering system are numerous, but this is one the major benefits for restaurants. Think about it this way—there are people (especially in the younger generation) who are going to choose the food they eat based on what they can order online. You may think that sounds ridiculous, but it's true. An increasing number of people would prefer to not have to pick up a phone, instead preferring to peruse and order from a menu at their leisure online. If you don't have an online ordering system, then you're missing out on this market. You will still get calls from those who continue to pick up the phone and call in their orders, but you won't get any orders from those that don't—and why wouldn't you want to tap into that extended market and expand your reach?

2. Ease of use

These days, most people would rather order online than picking up a phone. They have the menu right in front of them and the ability to make substitutions or additions. They can take their time. Long gone are the days where you had to get everyone's order together before calling (or deciding what you want on the phone, which is always a nightmare for restaurants).

Now, customers can pass around a mobile device to let everyone choose what they want, they can review the order without worrying that the person on the other end of the line entered something wrong, and they can pay immediately without having to recite their credit card number.

The bottom line is that by offering online ordering, you're giving your customers an easier way to order delivery or take out. On top of that, it's easier for your restaurant to be able to look at an order that came directly from the site and the customer. There is none of that "what does this say?" and there is no missing out on additional request like "well done" or "extra tomatoes" that can come back as a complaint if ignored by the person taking the order over the phone.

3. Dynamic and useful features

To put it simply, ordering online is just more fun. Aside from being able to have the menu right in front of you and add and remove items as you please, there are a ton of features you can implement to enhance the overall experience. For example, Domino's Pizza Tracker app builds a pizza in front of your eyes as you add toppings. Once an order is placed, the tracker lets the customer know at what stage of the preparation and delivery process their pizza is in. Like Domino's, you can even add an area where customers can supply feedback. You can also implement loyalty programs that are run straight through the website with little work on your part.

4. Tracking and analytics

With online ordering comes better tracking and analytics, and the best part is that the website or app will basically do everything for you. You know that it's important to measure and track success, and having an online ordering system can help. It can aid you in figuring out which coupons work and which don't, and it lets you easily receive feedback from your patrons. So what are you waiting for? Implement that online ordering and get tracking and growing!

Rev Up Sales with a Online Ordering System

Where are your customers? Sure, you might point out to your dining area and say, "They're right there," but that's only part of it. How did those customers find your restaurant? Most of the time, new customers come to your place through one of two ways—suggestions from a peer or from an online search. The internet is extremely important today, and many restaurants are starting to discover that it's about far more than just getting a better page ranking.

Quite a few are offering online restaurant ordering. They do this for pickup and delivery orders, as well as to start an order before someone arrives at the restaurant. This is common with large parties, for example. Being able to order online is very convenient and should be easy for the customer. Here are some tips to ensure that your online ordering is as simple as possible for your customers.

1. Easy to find

First, you have to make sure that the customers who visit your website are able to see how and where to order online. You need to have a large button that is easy to see right away. If they have to hunt and search to find out where to order, they will likely just choose another restaurant. Placing it in the upper left corner is a good location, but you can experiment with your site to see which one works the best for you. Also, make it stand out from the rest of the text and graphics on the page. Even making it a contrasting color can do the trick.

2. A legible menu

When people are ordering, they want to be able to go through your menu and understand what it is they are getting! Make the menu easy to read with large and legible letters—do not use fancy fonts. Separate the menu into different item types so the user can find what he or she wants quickly and easily. The descriptions themselves need to be very clear as well.

3. Include transparent pricing

Customers want to know exactly how much they will be paying before they get to the payment page. Your online ordering application needs to keep a running total of the bill, including the tax and delivery fee if applicable. This needs to be easy to see, and if it follows the customer from page to page, even better. The Domino's Pizza Tracker app is an excellent example of this.

4. Use online payments and tips

Your site should be able to take online payments as well. Many people carry very little cash with them today. Instead, they prefer to pay with their debit or credit cards, so you should certainly make this an option for your customers. In addition to paying for the cost of the food, make it possible to add a gratuity right onto the total. This way, they do not have to scrounge for money to pay a delivery driver a tip, and they don't have to write it on the receipt, which they may forget to note when they are balancing their account later. Instead, it should all be taken care of in the main transaction.

5. Remember mobile

As important as it is to have a quality website with an easy to use order form, you also have to think about going mobile. Much of the world today relies on their smartphones and tablets for most of their computing needs. They are certainly using them when they are ordering food online.

Having a high quality online restaurant ordering system in place can be a great way to increase your sales without having to increase your overhead because it all goes to your bottom line. But don't think about it in terms of the future, it's what today's customers expect.

4 Things Food Trucks Teach Us About Innovation

You would be hard pressed to find a city in America today that doesn't have its fair share of trendy food trucks traversing its streets. One cannot dispute that these tasty treats-on-wheels have won the hearts of Americans from coast to coast. So what can restaurants learn from these agile and adept entrepreneurs?

1. Adapt...then move on

Part of the food truck mystique is the seasonal fare they offer to their patrons. Dishes are often based on the constantly changing local ingredients with most ingredients being sourced locally. Understandably, the availability of many ingredients fluctuates with the weather and other uncontrollable factors. Food truck proprietors meet these challenges by changing menu items almost daily. You don't have to change your menu daily, but you may want to consider adding seasonal fare as a special on a weekly or bi-weekly basis. Menu mainstays will always have their following, but you might be surprised by the following your new menu items will develop as well. Eventually, you may find that your clientele comes exclusively seeking a seasonal menu item. This is a low risk way to experiment with your menu and capitalize immediately or fail immediately. Either way, your investment of time and money is small making the potential reward worth the risk.

2. Start with what you know

What makes food trucks awesome is that they offer just a few items that are really delicious. Starting with a solid base and adding in a little experimentation can produce incredible flavors and profitable results. Innovation doesn't have to be complicated to be great—a fresh take on the familiar can be just as groundbreaking as something brand new.

3. Make it personal

Although not as expensive as opening a traditional restaurant, a food truck requires an initial investment of $5,000 to $10,000 and countless hours. This means that the company's success is financially and emotionally personal for many owners. If you already own or operate an establishment, consider baby stepping your way into the food truck arena with a to-go counter or window that stays open after hours. You may even want to consider lowering the prices on items sold there. It will open you up to an entirely new clientele and will thrill your regular patrons.

4. Behold the power of partnerships

Many food truck businesses see more consistent sales when two or more trucks offering complementary foods pair up. Why not do the same? Think about other restaurants that offer complimentary products and invite them to hand out samples or provide some type of special for your patrons. Promote each other on your websites. Send out a special offer to each other's database. Don't think of every other restaurant as a competitor. Think of them as potential partners and seek out ways to leverage your strengths and capitalize on your differences.

5 Tips for Building Your Restaurant's Marketing Plan

In today's competitive landscape, it's not enough to have a great concept, excellent location, top chef, trending menu and impeccable service. To be successful, you must also communicate with customers to get (and keep) them coming through your doors. You must invest in marketing

Developing and executing a marketing plan may seem like a daunting task, but it's critical to building your brand and ensuring your restaurant get noticed and your tables filled. Here are a few tips to help you get started:

1. **Find your niche and promote it**

The most common way to do this in this industry is through public relations (PR). PR differs from advertising in that its goal is to persuade potential customers and influencers, among others, to have a specific opinion about your restaurant via the managed spread of information, traditionally the press. To get the press to write about you, you need to give them a reason to.

What do you want to be known for, perhaps a theme day or a monthly wine dinner? For example, an upscale restaurant known for its avant-garde wine list offered $3 tasting portions of every wine on its list on Monday nights. Not only did this provide a great opportunity for customers to try wines with very little risk, it also brought them in on an otherwise slow night and gave the press something to talk about.

Decide what your specialty is and spread the word. Don't forget about bloggers in addition to traditional media. Bloggers are the new influencers; research suggests over 70% of consumers will make a purchase based upon a review from a trusted blogger.

2. Decide if you need to hire a professional

There are so many ways to get your message out and the strategy you choose depends largely on the size and reach of your business. Are you a small restaurant focused on your local community or are you a multi-outlet business targeting a much larger geography? Do you, or one of your employees, have the ability and time to take on this task? If not, an independent consultant can take over those tasks that you don't have the time or skill set for.

Perhaps you just need a little guidance. There are many excellent online resources. Entreprenuer.com has a great How To for writing a press release that will get noticed as well as tips for speaking with reporters and how to select publications to target. Determine your needs, assess your resources, set a budget and monitor your return on the investment (business generated less cost incurred). You may be surprised by how much you gain for a relatively small investment.

3. **Engage customers on social media**

Customer engagement is the key to effective social media. Your goal should be to get consumers to join in your conversation and share your message to create a buzz for your business. Craft posts that will make people want to get involved and contribute in addition to posts that communicate your brand message and promote your business. Engaged fans can actually become marketers for your restaurant!

You can also use social media as part of your PR strategy. Reach out to the media via Twitter, as well as to groups who would be interested in your niche offering, i.e. wine clubs, food clubs, etc. (don't forget to follow, like and engage with these individuals in return). Include photos (professional photography not necessary) for visual appeal.

Post often, but DON'T overdo it, once a day should be sufficient—quality trumps quantity.

Use #hashtags, set up your geotag and maximize exposure by linking your posts across platforms. Remember people use different platforms in different ways. Twitter is conversational, while Facebook is about connecting with people and things you are interested in and Instagram is for sharing photos and videos in real time. Design and write your content based on the platform you will use. If you choose to use more than one, repurpose the same content in different ways according to the layout and preference for each site.

4. Create a website that is an expression of your restaurant

Your website provides 24/7 marketing and is one of the first elements you must have in place (even before your grand opening)! You cannot *not* have a great website, but a great website does not have to come at great cost. There are many online services that offer templates (some designed specifically for the restaurant industry) and hosting for free or nominal fees.

Whatever you do, be sure to use a responsive template, meaning your website will automatically adjust for the device the customer uses to view it on. There are also services that will construct and maintain the site for you.

Consider hiring a professional photographer as your photos need to entice customers to want to eat your food. When designing your site, keep in mind it should be a reflection of your establishment and the experience diners can expect. Include the following and keep your content up to date:

- Your menu
- Pictures of your restaurant
- Pictures of your food
- An "About Us" section
- Contact information
- Reservation policy
- Delivery information, if applicable

Last but not least, remember search engine optimization (SEO) when crafting your content. The internet a treasure trove of information on this subject. A quick Google search will pull up all the information you'll need to get started. If you don't have time, you may want to consider hiring a consultant to handle it for you.

5. Traditional advertising may work if you choose less expensive options

Traditional advertising, such as newspaper advertising, can be expensive and limit how much you can do. Look to local neighborhood newspapers as a less expensive options. As a bonus, a local newspaper may reach more of the customers you want versus a large metro one. You can also promote special offers for your local customers to show your appreciation of their patronage and to encourage loyalty. Keep creative costs down by repurposing photographs from your website and ask if they provide design services for a small fee (or free).

While marketing may seem like an intimidating task, focusing on the five key elements reviewed above and understanding the resources available will help your restaurant to get noticed over the competition and set you up for success.

10 Social Media Strategies to Help Market Your Restaurant

Social media has become an integral part of daily life for most Americans. Whether you own or manage a restaurant, social media may be the key to expanding your business and increasing your brand reputation. Here are 10 tips that can make it work for you.

1. Use hashtags

Hashtags are huge. They are both prevalent and relevant. Use trending hashtags to increase awareness about your business and your profile. Make sure to include relevant trending hashtags. If it is Margarita Monday, for example, make it #margaritamonday and post a picture of happy patrons enjoying their margaritas.

2. Use niche hashtags, too

Make sure your target market finds you by using specific hashtags. If you are new to Midtown Miami, for example, consider #midtownmojitos.

3. Embed videos

Take advantage of this tool. Provide video testimonials and interviews with your chef. You might want to film a happy hour or perhaps the preparation of an amazing meal.

4. Geo-target your ads

Geo-targeting allows both the diner and the establishment to see or search for businesses in their particular geographic location. You can also target your content to be delivered to those with specific likes and by those who like establishments such as your own. Nervous about the competition? Target their followers and offer incentives for them to try your place next time.

5. Run contests and promotions

Social promotions add excitement and keep customers and potential customers coming back to both your page—and your restaurant. Consider holding monthly or weekly contests and use your page to increase buzz and encourage people to visit.

6. Post exclusive offers

Conduct special promotions that provide a discount for anyone who likes or follows your page. Have servers inform patrons of it while they're on site. Customers will be grateful and more likely to return. Provide incentives for sharing your page.

7. Post lots of pictures that make your dishes look attractive

Images are some of the most shared posts on Facebook and they're the whole basis for sites like Instagram and Pinterest. Consider creating a look book of your current menu offerings.

8. Use page tabs to entice people into your establishment

Pay special attention to the first four tabs as they appear on the front page and don't need to be clicked to be seen.

9. Be all that you can be!!

Some social media sites provide 851-351 pixels where you can market your business for FREE. Make sure you use them. Be sure to include pictures of sumptuous food and people having a great time enjoying it. Update your cover image periodically to reflect new items, menu changes, seasonal fare and any specials.

10. **Maximize the potential of mobile social sites like Instagram**

People use these sites on their phones, so if you include location specificity in your tags, you may increase foot traffic by enticing patrons that are in your immediate vicinity.

Anyone in the restaurant industry can tell you that knowing your clientele is the key to growing your business. Social media provides you an opportunity to connect with your customers and market your business at the same time.

Use Content Marketing to Cultivate Relationships

The purpose of content marketing, or any marketing really, is to attract and keep customers. In order to keep existing customers and gain new ones, a restaurant needs to do something to attract, acquire, and engage new and existing clients. Content marketing is the process through which you create and distribute relevant and valuable information to your restaurant's current and potential diners.

When done correctly, content marketing allows you to engage your audience and provide them with something of value, making them want to return to your restaurant or try it for the first time.

Think of content marketing as brand management. When developing a strategy, support your restaurant brand's message by creating and sharing relevant content. If you don't have a content marketing strategy, it's time to develop one or hire someone to do so for you. The reality is that content marketing costs 62% less than traditional marketing and generates about three times as many leads. You can't afford not to invest in it.

Content marketing strategies allows you to create a connection with current and potential customers that inspires them to return again and again. Your establishment will become more than a coupon, it becomes a mainstay in their lives. Content humanizes your brand and makes you approachable. It is easily shareable and it allows you to re-use and re-purpose marketing materials and images in new, unique and effective ways.

1. Define your strategies and goals

Your strategy should be to build a relationship with your guests in order to drive more traffic to your restaurant and your website.

2. Create a timeline

Do this one month at a time. Design the content of your marketing around seasonal events like holidays and festivals. Make sure to post your calendar and share it with restaurant staff. Make sure your calendar is easily accessible via your emails, company website and blogs. Post it on social media and share as often as you can.

3. Make content outlines

Outlining your content allows you to cross promote across various avenues and create a unified look so your brand is easily identifiable.

4. **Define your voice**

Be authentic and exciting. Use a combination of text, images and video. What kind of personality does your business have? Let it shine through in your content.

5. **Re-purpose content**

You don't have to "recreate the wheel" for each avenue. Use television commercials on YouTube. Link to your blog content on social media and through your email news. Spruce up old images by adding them to new content. Basically, use what you've got.

6. **Optimize your content**

Use keywords and optimize your images by including alternative tags. Alt tags describe the image when the image can't be displayed. Also make sure your title tags are optimized. Reduce your image file size (without sacrificing quality) for faster-loading web pages.

7. **Put someone in charge**

You don't have to create all of your content, but you should oversee it at least in the beginning. Just make sure that there is one specific person who is tasked with content management and quality control.

8. **Track and measure**

Ensure you are tracking your content. Get feedback from your audience. Consistently monitor your progress. Adjust your tactics when you don't get a favorable response. Installing Google Analytics on your website is easy (and FREE!) way to track important KPIs that will help you gauge your success.

Chapter 4 Reflection

WHAT WILL YOU TAKE FROM THIS CHAPTER TO ADAPT TO YOUR PROFIT RECIPE?

_____

_____

_____

WHAT ARE THE TOP 3 ACTIONS YOU ARE GOING TO TAKE AS A RESULT OF THIS CHAPTER?

1. _____

   _____

2. _____

   _____

3. _____

   _____

Chapter 5: The Time is Now!

2020 Is Closer Than It Seems

I started this book by telling you that being in the food industry sucks your time, energy, and money, leaving you with very little rewards in return. It is also one of the most rewarding, fun, and challenging businesses to be in. I believe it is one filled with unbelievable opportunities for those that are willing to work hard, but most importantly, work smart.

In recent months, we've seen San Francisco based food delivery service Munchery raise $28 million, on-demand delivery infrastructure Postmates raise $16 million, and lunch and dinner on demand App Sprig each raise about $10 million. See a theme here?

You could jump on a food delivery service bandwagon using a service like GrubHub, Caviar or Seamless and compete with a bunch of other restaurants that they promote, plus give them a chunk of your profit and margin, but why? Why do that when you can do it yourself?

I hope that by reading this book you realize that giving away your profits is not a formula for long-term success. What is?

Create a lifestyle brand to add recurring customers +
Control and automate your process +
Add an off-premise component to offer more convenience +
More PROFIT in your pocket!

I wrote this book so I could give you a roadmap to help guide you to success before 2020 is here. I've shared the costly, time consuming mistakes I made when starting out and what I would have done differently had I known better. I've laid out the realities of running a food business so you go in with your eyes wide open and can develop a strategy to overcome the challenges of rising food and labor costs, employee issues, and customers wanting more for less all in an extremely competitive environment.

I've shared important trends that are shaping the industry and how you can take advantage of them. I've provided you with checklists and processes to determine where to focus to create new revenue streams for your business.

At the end of each chapter, I've asked you to identify what your key take aways from each chapter are, as well as the top 3 actions you are going to take as a result so you can create a focused action plan.

I hope you did the thinking and wrote out your actions items. If so, you probably found tremendous value while reading the book and built out your Profit Recipe. Most importantly, I want you to spring into action to build a successful, profitable business in the food industry.

What I don't want is for this to be another book that gets you excited and motivated, but that doesn't alter anything for you. As the old saying goes: "You can lead a horse to water, but you can't make him drink."

The food industry is going through a transformative time and you are in a tremendous position to take advantage of this while your competition stays stuck in old ways of doing things. You have the information, and you have the tools and resources. Now you just need to take action. Go do it!

CHAPTER 6: THE PROFIT RECIPE

Action Items: Ingredients for Success

- Leave a review on **Amazon**

- Sign up to our newsletter to get monthly updates and research http://www.theprofitrecipe.com/blogs/

- Sign up for a webinar to understand different delivery models

- Schedule a consultation call to address your Q&A with Cesar

- Join our community and share ideas on Facebook

- Follow us on Twitter to keep yourself informed

- Connect on LinkedIn and ask Cesar any question

- Subscribe to our YouTube channel

ACKNOWLEDGEMENTS

I've read a lot of books during my journey, and I've always been amazed at the amount of people that were thanked. But after taking this adventure and trying to put my thoughts into words, I realized it really takes a village... In my case, Wendy Lieber was the village leader. Thank you for making this book a reality and going through it with me!

I would like to thank my parents for teaching me the meaning of hard work, the importance of values and how going against the crowd is mostly a good thing when you're following your vision. To my twin sister Nani, you have been my rock throughout the years and I have been blessed to grow up with you. I'm also grateful to my band of brothers: Carlos, the romantic philosophical businessman; Andy, the financial straight-shooter; and Mickey, the peace-maker and joy of the house.

To my inspirations, Luly B and Ralph Quintero for showing me that it can be done and inspiring me to follow your path.

To my Fit2Go customers, colleagues and friends that have made me become the person I am today and have seen me go through the business roller coaster that has helped me learn from my mistakes:
Aaron Lee, Alejandro Mora, Amaloha Orejuela, Ana Martinez, Andrea Gonzalez, Armando Armenta, Andreina Vidal, Andres Betancourt, Arnold Kovelman, Carolina Antonini, Carolina Berardi, Celia Meza, David Redlich, David Sosman, Dean Schwartz, Delia Barreto, Doug Barra, Eloise Gonzalez, Felipe Guzman, Grace Carricarte, Heather Schweitzman, Ian Brillembourg, Ivan Hernandez, Jason Alpert, Jason Schweitzman, Javier Contreras, Jackie de Nichols, Jaime Yordan-Frau, Javier Saborio, Jody Johnson, John Fazio, Juan Lavista, Julie Laberge, Karla Faundez, Keyla Lazardi, Kris High, Kyle Lochridge, Lauren Haro, Lazaro Oliva, Leonard Goldberg, Leslie Herrera, Lily Balepogi, Luis Luciani, Mark Nelson, Maya Perez de Diaz, Patricia Lyons, Patricia Q. de Armenta, Phil Stevenson, Preston Dickerson, Rebecca Amster, Ricardo Trillos, Roberto Hollander, Rodulfo Prieto, Sal D'Elia, Sandra

Millor, Sara Weston, Scott Fritz, Scott Kent, Sebastian Mangiavillano, Shary Thur, Steven Koslowski, Valerie Major, Victor Ridaura, Yanet Arevalo, and Yuen Yung.

Finally, I want to thank the person that supports me and loves me unconditionally, no matter what adventure we go through; my wife Patricia. Thank you for believing in me and allowing me to be the entrepreneur I was born to be. To my daughter Isabella, whose eyes and energy can fill my life forever, this book is for you: my reason to be.

About the Author

Cesar Quintero works with Foodpreneurs who want to expand their successful concept and improve their margins using the current industry trends. He shares his experience of 11 years in the Food Business to help them make more money and avoid costly mistakes. He also speaks at Food Summits and Restaurant Conventions about disruptive models and up-to-date trends in the market.

His passion for independence, business and food has shaped his entire life. He graduated as a Production Engineer that specializes in process management and logistics. He then worked for Procter and Gamble (P&G) for three years as a marketing manager for Latin America.

In 2005, he moved to Miami given the economic turmoil in Venezuela to pursue his dream of starting a business and helping others achieve a healthier lifestyle by founding Fit2Go. His experience as a production engineer shifted Fit2Go's original concept of a Local Healthy Café to a more innovative and effective Healthy Meal Delivery Service that would leverage on technology and logistics to satisfy the needs of health conscious professionals.

In 2013 Quintero graduated from the MIT Entrepreneurship Masters Program and founded two new companies: RawBar2Go (the first licensed food boat in Florida) and The Profit Recipe (a coaching and leasing software platform to help restaurants add a delivery component to their brick & mortar models).

Made in the USA
Lexington, KY
14 February 2017